The Police on the Go

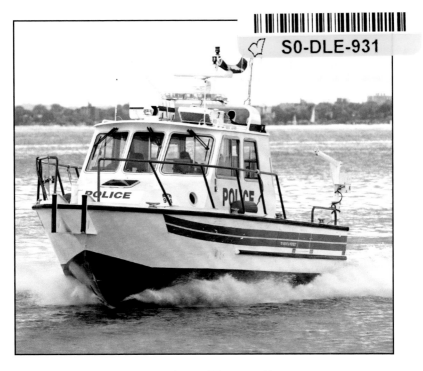

S0-DLE-931

by Kris Bonnell

The police can go in a car.

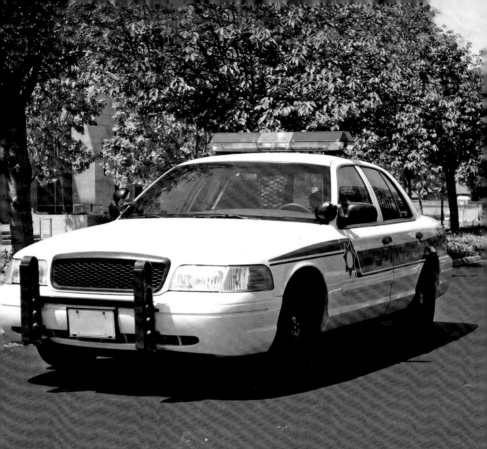

The police can go on a bike.

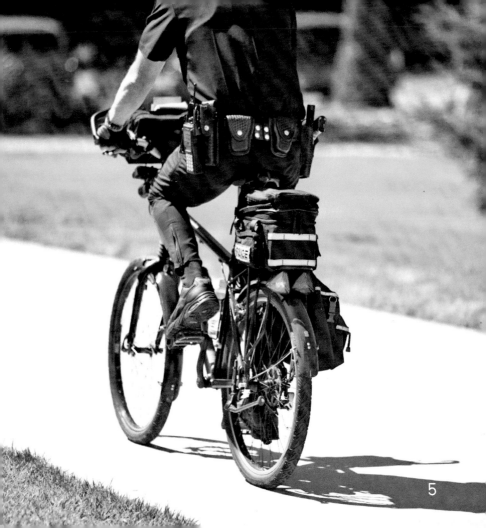

The police can go in a helicopter, too.

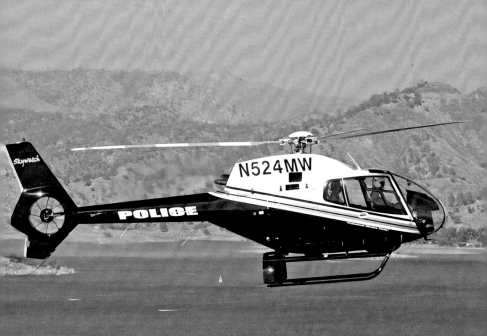

The police can go on a motorcycle.

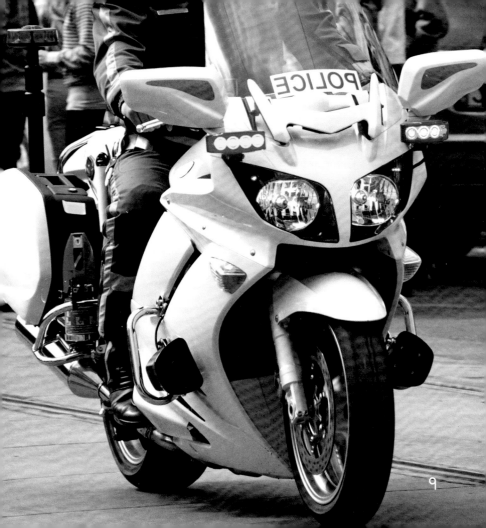

The police can go on a boat.

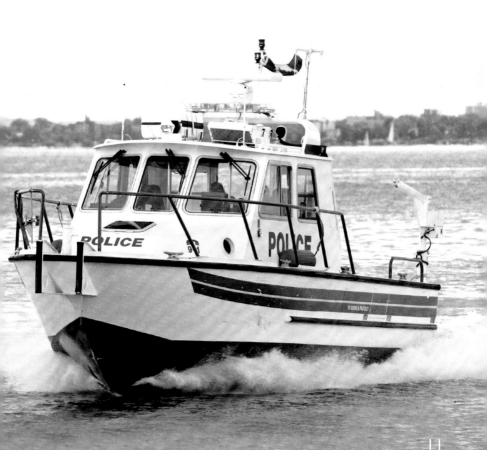

The police can go
on a horse, too.

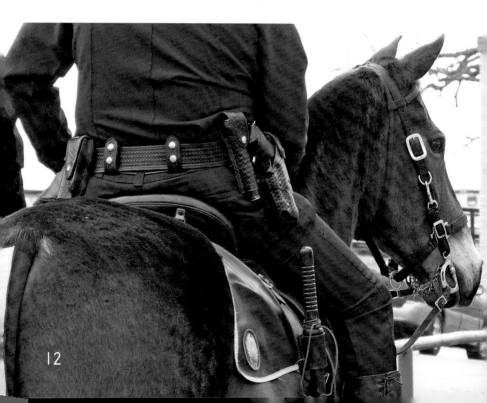